OUT OF DARKNESS INTO LIGHT

One Woman's Journey from Death to Life

Morgan Swartz

ISBN 979-8-89112-088-4 (Paperback)
ISBN 979-8-89112-089-1 (Digital)

Covenant Books
11661 Hwy 707
Murrells Inlet, SC 29576
www.covenantbooks.com

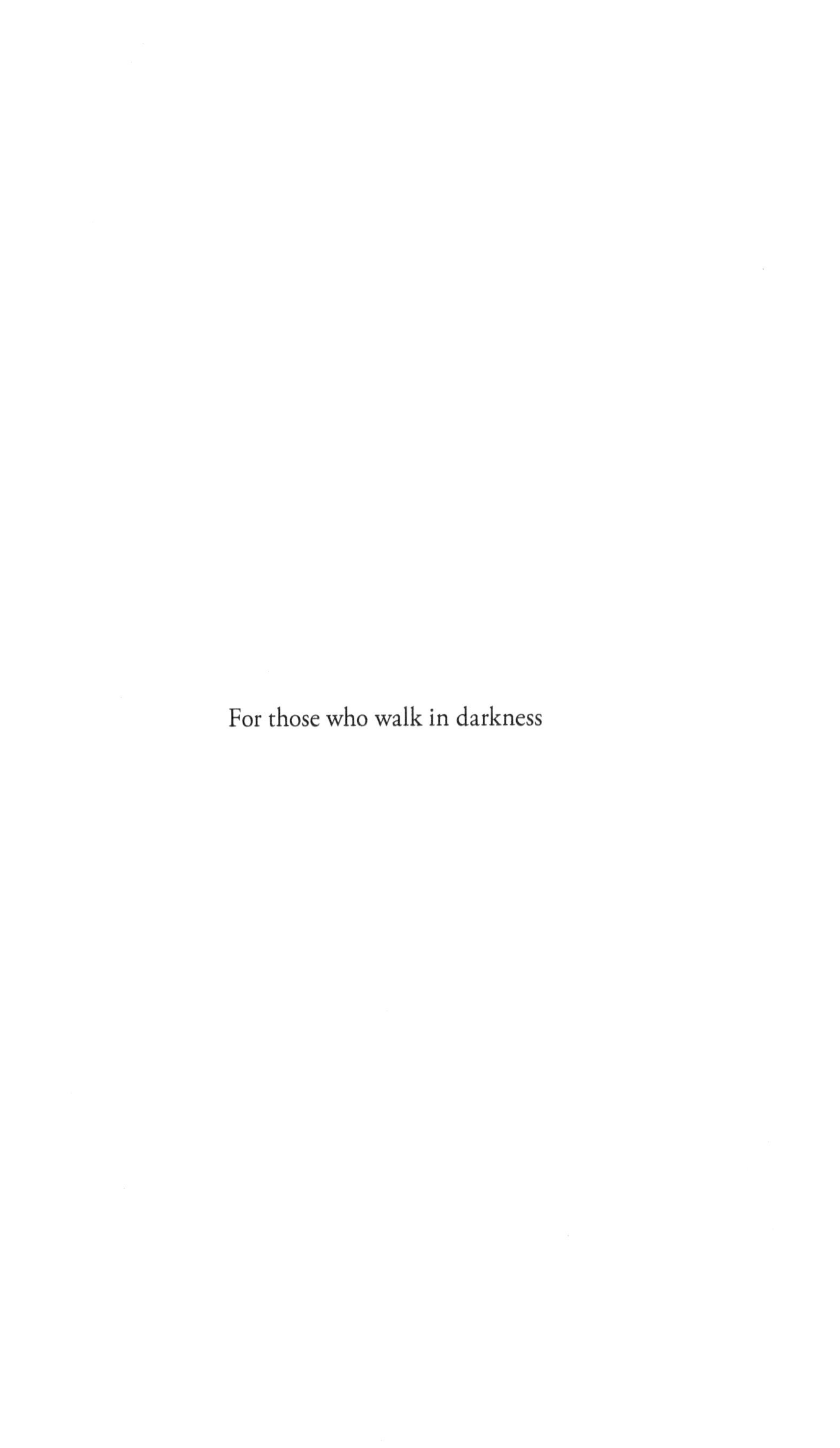

For those who walk in darkness

Totus Tuus Maria Ego Sum,

Ad Majorem Dei Gloriam.

The light shines in the darkness, and the
darkness has not overcome it.

—John 1:5 (RSVCE)

CONTENTS

OUT OF DARKNESS

This is a story about light—specifically, the light of Christ—and how it has manifested itself in my life. It seems to me that this light can't be fully understood unless we first consider its counterpart, the dark. The things that leave us feeling frightened and crying out for "Aunty Em." The times when we feel most helpless and alone, when it seems like it's never going to get better, like no one cares, like we're in a deep, dark tunnel with no way out.

I could go on a theological rant about the purpose of suffering in salvation, but I won't. Those books already exist, and they sit on my shelves, collecting dust. Why would I want to read about why it's good that I'm suffering when I don't want to suffer? Besides, God is infinitely simple, and since I'm made in His image and likeness, I believe He's created me the same way. Plus, when God wants to get something across to me, He meets me where I am. It just so happens that He often finds me at the movie theater.

I love movies. Growing up, one of my favorite pastimes was popping a VHS tape into my family's VCR and getting lost in the film. My soul was always transcended by the beauty, truth, and goodness I found there. If it was a really good film, I'd find myself in what I dubbed a "movie coma" come the credits, curled up in a ball and unable to move because I was so affected by what I'd witnessed.

I've learned many valuable life lessons from movies. The summer following my freshman year in college, the Disney/Pixar film

Inside Out was released in theaters. I've always been a big Disney buff, so I didn't shy away from an invitation to see the movie for free—even if it was with my eight-year-old cousin and her friends. We plopped down in front of the huge screen, popcorn in hand, brimming with excitement.

The plot was pretty simple: a young girl named Riley moved across the country with her parents and had to adapt to her new surroundings, standard stuff. What made the film unique, though, was that we were watching it from the viewpoint of Riley's emotions—namely Joy, Sadness, Anger, Fear, and Disgust. Each emotion was personified by a tiny pixelated character whose main personality trait was their given emotion. The movie was narrated by the bright, bubbly Joy. It was clear that she was the ringleader of Riley's emotions. Joy called the shots, and her goal was to avoid any negativity from entering Riley's mind. This led Joy to have a particular distaste for Sadness.

At first, all I could think was, *Sadness is such a drag! She's constantly holding Joy back, getting in the way of good things, and pointing out the bad.* Even her mannerisms irked me. Sadness moved slowly, hardly ever stood upright, and was often face down on the ground wallowing in self-pity. Not once did I pause to consider her subtle, positive qualities, like her serious demeanor that helped Riley make more prudent decisions. I also failed to take into account Sadness's incredible empathy, ability to work hard in the face of adversity, and Christlike compassion.

I realized I'd been doing the same thing as this fictional character for as long as I could remember. Rather than make peace with the dark parts of my past, I'd been trying to hide them out of fear they would prevent my joy from ever returning. Yet as a pivotal scene in the movie made apparent, sadness is never meant to have the final say; it always leads to joy.

It's like St. Paul wrote to the Romans, "We know that all things work for good for those who love God, who are called according to His purpose" (Romans 8:28). This lie I'd been holding onto for so long often kept me from telling my story—at least, it prevented me from sharing the parts that weren't pretty. There were times when I felt so far gone that I wondered if I would ever see the light again. But what I've learned about the darkness is that the only way out is through.

Let's step out of the darkness together, shall we?

DOUBTING MORGAN

"We're moving!"

While this may have scared some kids, I was ecstatic when my parents made the announcement in the spring of 2007. My parents had dreamed of building their own home for years. Now—three kids later—their dream was becoming a reality.

"Yep. And you and Erin will have your own rooms! How does that sound?"

How did that sound? Like *my* dream was coming true! It's not like I didn't love my little sister, but when there's a six-year age gap, it's nice to have your own space.

For the first ten years of my life, I lived on Deer Run Lane. I always thought it was a dumb name since I didn't see many deer running around, just kids. We had several neighbors in our forested subdivision, all of whom had children. The family at the end of the street even had identical twin girls. They were a year older than me, and we had gotten fairly close over the years. We rode the bus to school together and would often ride bikes after we all got home. I remember being in awe of the twins, who could ride their bikes down the hills without holding onto their handlebars. I would watch them ride with their arms outstretched, their blonde hair flying in the wind— fearless. They seemed inseparable and unstoppable. I wondered what it would be like to have a twin. You could take on the world side by side, and nothing would be able to stop you. Or would it?

~ ~ ~

Less than a year prior to the announcement of our move, I received another wave of good news. I was in the school cafeteria, waiting to be picked up by my mom. Dozens of screaming kids darted in and out among the long wooden tables, much to the dismay of the teachers who were telling us to sit down. When I saw my mom come in, something on her face told me to stay in my seat. She didn't look panicked or anything, but there was an energy exuding from her that seemed to electrocute everyone in close proximity. It was like the Red Sea parting for her, and she was able to make a beeline for me without scathing a single child.

Mom had her cell phone up to her ear. If I were to guess who she was talking to, it was probably my grandma. But today, she didn't seem to be having a grandma conversation; this seemed like a Morgan-we-just-won-a-million-dollars conversation. I was fully prepared to spend my earnings on sending all the other kids to a different school. When she finally drew up next to me, Mom seemed too excited to speak. "Mary has something to tell you," was all she got out before thrusting the phone in my hand.

Outside my immediate family, my Aunt Mary was the person I was closest to while growing up. Being my mom's older sister and my godmother, Mary was around a lot in the first few years of my life. I was the only grandchild at the time and the focus of everyone's attention, especially Mary's. She loved to babysit me, play with me, and take me on outings. Even if I was too little to remember the details, I remember being enthralled by my aunt. At times, it seemed like she was the center of my world. I thought nothing could come between us, not even my baby brother, who was about to make his big debut.

As fate would have it, it wasn't my brother I had to worry about, but another man. Mary moved halfway across the country with him when I was only two years old. Though it didn't work out between them, she met another guy while in North Carolina and settled down to start a family there. Though I couldn't have located it on a map, I felt a divide between us wider than the Cumberland Gap. I didn't know how—or if—such a severance could be bridged. I had lost my closest companion, and I didn't think anyone would be able to replace her.

~ ~ ~

"We're having twin girls, and we want to name one after you!"

I was speechless. I'd never given much thought to my name; whenever I did, I would usually come to the conclusion that I didn't care for it. I thought it would be nice to be named something spicier, like "Michelle," or super-extra, like "Adelaide." Let me tell you, your name starts to sound a lot nicer when someone says they're naming their firstborn after you.

"And the babies are going to be born in May, right around your birthday! What do you think about all that, sweetie?"

What did I think? I couldn't think. I was so excited that I was incapable of forming a coherent thought. I started seeing doubles: two strollers, two car seats, and two cousins to love. Two bridges. It was all too much.

I probably talked about it at school to the point where people wanted to punch me in the face. But I didn't care; my godmother was having twins, and there was nothing anyone could do about it.

~ ~ ~

"It's called what?"

"Twin-to-twin transfusion syndrome."

"But what does that mean?"

"It means we really have to pray for Mary and the babies now," my mom told me.

Only a short while into her pregnancy, Mary was diagnosed with a medical condition that none of us had ever heard of, much less anticipated playing a role in our family that would shake the foundations of our faith and change the course of our lives forever.

I quickly learned that twin-to-twin transfusion syndrome (TTTS) occurs when a woman is pregnant with twins but only has one placenta. This makes it difficult for both babies to receive the proper amount of nutrients. I don't know the exact statistics, but I was told there was a chance one or both of my cousins would not survive. This was a devastating blow for us all; I became overwhelmed by a feeling of helplessness, so I did the only thing I could—pray.

I think my family owes our Catholic faith in a large part to my great-grandmother, Shirley Huck, who was always referred to as "Granny." Granny Huck was a fiercely faithful and incredibly resilient woman. Forced to grow up in a day and age where there were world wars and great depressions, life quickly taught her to hold her own. I remember my mom telling the story of how Granny had given birth to her first child, my grandma. Granny's mother—my great-great-grandma—had come into the house, put a stick between Granny's teeth, and told her, "The neighbors better not hear a thing." Needless to say, the women in my family have a history of being extreme.

Granny drew a great deal of strength from her faith. She had many special devotions, and her greatest love—after God and PawPaw Huck, of course—was St. Thérèse of Lisieux. Granny had a small statue of this saint in her bedroom, and after she died, PawPaw had a larger statue of St. Thérèse placed in our parish chapel in memory of my great-grandma. My great-grandparents' devotion to St. Thérèse was profound, but I only learned why long after they were gone. Apparently, PawPaw Huck almost died on the way home from serving in World War II; his appendix burst on the ship, and he developed peritonitis. When Granny received the word that her fiancé was dying, she begged St. Thérèse to intercede for their cause. She promised to name their first daughter Thérèse if this saint would ask God to spare my great-grandpa. Within two years of Granny's request, my great-grandparents were married and my grandmother was born. Her name? Therese.

~ ~ ~

I have a vague memory of praying the rosary with Mary beside Granny's hospice bed. Granny had developed lung cancer, and we knew her time was short. Though I don't remember being especially close with my great-grandma, we went to her house a lot, especially in her final days. I felt superfluous and small sitting on the floor in the front room while my family took turns talking to Granny as she passed in and out of consciousness. Sometimes I would wander around the house, eating the ever-present Oreos in the kitchen or playing with the stacks of cards in the basement. I would always find my way back to their bedroom, where I would stare at the little statue of St. Thérèse.

I wondered what she really looked like. Her brown habit, black veil, and white whatever-it-was-called seemed so cumbersome. Not to mention that it wasn't exactly stylish; I wondered if it had been back then. I couldn't imagine such an entourage would have been comfortable, but the statue didn't seem to mind. Her face was serene, and she had a small smile on her face. I didn't know how she could be smiling at a time like this.

I was grateful when Mary broke into my reverie by peeking her head in the door.

"Want to pray the rosary with me?" she asked.

Her invitation made me feel special and important, knowing we had the ability to call on a higher power like Granny and Thérèse did. Though we wept while we prayed, I experienced a tremendous sense of comfort as I ran my fingers over the rosary beads and recited the familiar words.

My aunt was actually named after the Blessed Virgin Mary, whom we honor when we recite the rosary. Because of this, my godmother will always have a special connection to the Blessed Mother. Mary must have sensed this closeness because she and her husband, Bob, decided to entrust their pregnancy to Our Lady. I recall a slideshow Bob compiled of the twins when they were in utero, where ultrasound images of "Baby A" and "Baby B" flashed to the tune of "Let It Be" by The Beatles. I had never heard the song before but was struck by the lines *"When I find myself in times of trouble, Mother Mary comes to me. Speaking words of wisdom, let it be."*

I wasn't familiar with the inspirations of the Spirit at that point, but when I heard that song, I felt a fire start to burn inside me. It was as if God—who had once sent His only Son to save the world—was now sending His mother to comfort me and my family in our hour of need. There was a still small voice telling me to let go, to "let it be," promising everything would be all right.

Around the time they shared the slideshow, Mary and Bob told me they were naming their first daughter after the Blessed Mother instead of me. I thought it was fitting, given my newfound appreciation of the Virgin Mary. Besides, I wanted to give credit where credit was due; in the tradition of the Catholic Church, May is her month anyway.

~ ~ ~

You know the saying "April showers bring May flowers"? Well, not that year. The afternoon of May 1 was undecidedly overcast. You couldn't tell if the clouds were going to part and make way for the sun or if it was about to pour. The weather left me feeling wary as if nature itself was holding its breath.

I had a play practice after school that day. I was immersed in rehearsal and had nothing else on my mind for an entire hour. That all changed when I walked outside and saw my dad driving the van. Dad never picked us up from school; plus, he always drove the truck. My heart sank.

I didn't want to hone in on the dark thoughts I'd been pushing away for months. I didn't want to think of reasons why my mom wasn't there or what was causing the knot in my stomach and the lump in my throat. I stood, frozen and fearful, desperately wanting to rewind to the day when I'd walked out the same door to the news Mary was expecting twin girls. For a moment, it felt like I was still in rehearsal, like I was playing the lead in someone else's life. But this time, I didn't want to know the ending.

~ ~ ~

Mary Katherine McClurg was born on May 1, 2007. Her sister, Ellie Katherine, followed close behind. They were identical, except that one had a heartbeat and one was in heaven. Everything had been fine the week before. We were going to build a new house. I was going to get my own room. Mary was going to have twins. None of us understood how this could have happened.

Mary had two appointments every week leading up to the delivery date, which had been scheduled as a C-section for May 8. These checkups always involved an ultrasound; in addition to providing images of the babies, the ultrasound displayed ECGs to check their heartbeats. We had long since breathed sighs of relief since the girls had been doing well for months. Mary's final appointments were scheduled for May 1 and May 4. They'd had the option to deliver the girls at the end of April but had chosen to wait to give their lungs more time to develop. There was no way they could have known.

~ ~ ~

"Where's Mom?"

At first, my dad didn't say anything. He just stared straight ahead, struggling to find the right words. We pulled out of the parking lot and sped along to the home of Seth's friend, where he'd gone after school that day. I didn't dare speak; I was afraid of what my father would tell me. After picking up Seth, our next stop was getting Erin from day care. Dad said he would tell us everything once we were all together.

I don't remember how the conversation went, but I know it happened in the car. I have vivid memories of crying my eyes out in the front seat, unable to process what had happened. As my dad drove home, I stared at myself in the side-view mirror, tears streaming down my face. My entire body shook as the weight of what this meant for our family came crashing down on me.

Why, God, why? I screamed in my head. Silence.

"Objects in the mirror are closer than they appear," the mirror offered. *No kidding;* I scoffed. The truth of losing Mary Katherine was far too close; it was a possibility I pushed away for months. Now

it had become a reality, and the terrible truth was suffocating me. I couldn't think; I couldn't speak. All I could do was cry.

My grief became unbearable when Dad told us that Mom, her younger sister, Corie, and my grandparents had flown to North Carolina earlier that day to be with Mary and Bob. All I heard was that I had been left behind. I longed to weep with her—with my whole family—but instead, I felt abandoned, isolated, and alone. At the time, I couldn't see how God was working all things for good. I couldn't see past my own pain. I didn't understand the split-second decisions made by my mom and Corie. Perhaps they thought that bringing us kids would make things harder for Mary and Bob, who were now mourning the loss of a child. Maybe they thought seeing death up close would be traumatic for us. It's possible they couldn't afford the plane fare for everyone. Whatever the reason, this tragedy tore at my family—at least on one side.

We lived down the road from my dad's parents, so that night, he piled the three of us kids back into the van and drove to Nanny and Grandpa's to tell them the news. I don't know many people in my dad's extended family, so it caught me by surprise to find his god-father, Mark, there. Evidently, Mark had driven up from Springfield to visit for the day. This turned out to be providential, as Mark was an ob-gyn and was therefore all too familiar with TTTS. While Mary was blaming herself for Mary Katherine's death, Mark told us it wasn't anyone's fault.

"It just happens without any scientific reasons," he said softly, sharing in our loss.

While this proved to be a great source of comfort for my dad, I remained inconsolable. I didn't care about scientific reasons. I wanted divine answers. When I felt like God refused them over the following weeks, I welcomed the invitation to give Him the silent treatment. I also began to despise every set of twins I came into contact with, even those whom I had known long before my aunt had been preg-nant. It was agonizing to see identical twin girls, as they reminded me most of my cousins and how I felt robbed by God. I avoided the girls on my street like the plague. I couldn't wait until I moved away from them. I began pouring myself into anything that would take my mind off my pain: movies, music, and making plans for my new room. I couldn't let myself sit still too long, or I would descend into madness. The silence was deafening.

Soon, I stopped praying altogether. I didn't see the point. *Why should I talk to God if He won't talk to me?* I thought. Part of me didn't want to hear His answers. I couldn't see how anyone—not even Him—could explain why this tragedy had befallen my family. I started to wonder if God was even real. I remember someone saying to me around this time, "This is either going to break your faith or make it take off." I was far too angry at God to entertain the thought that Mary Katherine's death could somehow bring me closer to Him, so instead, I tried to push Him out of the picture completely. But I couldn't do it.

No matter how hard I tried, I couldn't fathom a life without God. Though I couldn't see His hand in the situation or feel His healing presence, I knew He was with me; I just *knew.* In the deepest, most real part of my being, I had to admit to myself that I believed in God—whether I liked Him or not at the moment. My feelings didn't change the fact that He loved me unconditionally—that He always has and always will.

Slowly, I began to see ways in which God brought good out of Mary Katherine's passing. One thing that dawned on me early on was that my cousin had hopefully gone straight to heaven. Not only did that mean eternal salvation for her, but it also meant a constant spiritual companion for me. There would be no waiting for her to grow up before we could become friends. We could communicate constantly. Being so close to Jesus and Mother Mary would render her able to intercede on behalf of our family; maybe she'd even invoke the help of St. Thérèse. Little did I know that this experience was about to take my devotion to saints to a whole new level.

~ ~ ~

In the Catholic Church, one of the seven sacraments is Confirmation. This sacrament is often referred to as a "personal Pentecost" and is seen as the completion of baptismal grace. In this way, the baptized are more perfectly bound to the Church. They are also enriched with the special strength of the Holy Spirit to go forth and spread the faith by word and deed. Part of a Catholic's preparation for Confirmation involves choosing a sponsor. This person should be someone who's been present in the candidate's life and whose faith is sincere, mature, and faithful to the Church's teachings. Though my godmother's faith had been severely tested by her daughter's death, Mary never lost sight of God, and I admired how devoted she was to Him and the Blessed Mother throughout her trials. I had always planned to ask Mary to be my sponsor, but after this experience, I knew without a doubt that she would be the one.

My confirmation would take place at the end of eighth grade. Months before I was to be confirmed, my religion teacher gave us books to read and discuss with our sponsors. Though my aunt was hundreds of miles away, she was dedicated to helping me prepare for this special sacrament. We carved out time each week to talk on the phone, and I treasured those times beyond words. I hadn't gotten to talk to Mary in what felt like forever since she'd become so busy taking care of Ellie. The deep, spiritual nature of our conversations was something new and incredibly meaningful for both of us. Then it came time to choose a patron saint, another part of Confirmation prep. I was told the saint's name would become part of my own. For example, if a kid in my class named John Michael Smith chose St. Sebastian, his new name would be John Michael Sebastian Smith. Our teacher said our saint should be someone we had something in common with or whose life we admired. Although I knew a few of my family members had devotions to certain saints, I wanted to choose a patron or patroness who meant something to me personally.

Since there were, quite literally, thousands of saints to choose from, I decided to narrow the playing field by pulling out my old saint book and making a list of the prettiest female ones. Dumb, I know, but God used that ridiculous ruse to lead me to Catherine of Siena. The first thing I noticed about St. Catherine, other than her looks, was her name. It immediately brought Mary Katherine to mind. I began reading about St. Catherine and was startled by the similarities I found between the two of us. Catherine was aware of

God's presence in the midst of terrible trials. She learned to lean on Him and trust Him more because of them, and she helped save the Church through her writings. She did this primarily by writing letters to the pope at the time, which helped prevent the Great Western Schism in the 1300s. Though I'd never corresponded with the pope, I knew I'd been blessed with the gift of writing and felt called to do great things with it for God. But what really sealed the deal was when I learned Catherine had something in common with my cousins: Catherine was a twin, and her twin had died at birth.

~ ~ ~

"I want my Confirmation name to be Catherine in honor of St. Catherine of Siena, but I'm going to spell it with a *K* in memory of Mary Katherine."

At first, I wasn't sure my aunt had heard me. There was silence on the other end of the line.

"Mary?"

Sniff. "Yes, sweetie?"

"Did you hear me?"

"Yes."

Now I could tell she was crying. It seemed she was as overwhelmed by the spiritual significance of the situation as I was.

"That means so much to me, Morgan. It's beautiful. I know Mary Katherine has a hand in all of this."

I knew it too. My cousin hadn't only bridged the decade-long divide between me and my aunt; she also paved the way for my patron saint, whose intercession I would soon see how desperately I needed.

THE DARK DAYS

"Ugh, it smells like old people in here." The comment wasn't entirely off base, as the building was almost a hundred years old, but I decided not to point that out to my classmate. Most guys in my eighth-grade class weren't too keen on having the obvious pointed out to them. I could never understand why. Something about thinking they were smarter than you?

Our class was forced to walk from our school building to the local Knights of Columbus Hall for our Confirmation retreat, though none of us knew what that meant. All we'd been told was that we wouldn't have classes that day. We could wear whatever we wanted (a rare occasion at a Catholic school), and we'd have pizza for lunch. For those reasons alone, I was pumped. When we first walked in, I heard music playing over the speakers. It wasn't weird religious music either; it was pop music. *Oh, no,* I thought. *Is this going to be another school thing where adults try to relate to us? That's always so awkward.* I gave the retreat team a once-over and was startled to find only two of them looked like...well, actual adults. The other three could have been college kids. Unlike most school assemblies, where the speakers were old and wore dress clothes, this bunch was clad in jeans and T-shirts. *Strange...*

"Hey, everybody! If you could find a seat, that'd be great. We'll get started in a couple of minutes."

The older guy seemed to be the spokesperson for the group. He seemed nice, but I was still skeptical. I was also less than thrilled to find we would be sitting in metal folding chairs all day. *This had better be good.*

"Thanks, everyone. My name's Paul, and I'm part of the team who will be presenting your retreat today."

Hm. Like St. Paul.

"I'm going to let the other team members introduce themselves, and then I'll tell you more about what you can expect from us."

Paul handed the microphone to one of his younger teammates, a girl with dark hair. I loved her simple style. She had her hair up and wore a blue flannel shirt with ballet flats. I sensed she would be my favorite.

"Hi, guys! I'm Rachel. I'm twenty-two, and I love Cardinals baseball and writing."

I couldn't have cared less about baseball, but I loved writing. *Maybe this retreat won't be as boring as I thought.* The rest of the team introduced themselves, and Paul was handed back the mic.

"We're going to mix it up today between fun and serious," Paul said, "and since we don't like to get serious right away, we're going to play a game."

He told us the competition would be between the guys and girls and would be similar to musical chairs—just way more intense. The room buzzed with excitement as we picked up our chairs and put them in a circle, per Paul's instructions. I kept glancing at Rachel, wondering how she planned to run around in flats. *She's my hero.* Before I knew it, we were off. Everyone was darting in and out among chairs, pulling people out of their seats, and laughing as classmates collided. The game put us all at ease, and I became more eager to hear what the presenters had to say.

Instead of leading with a talk, the team introduced each series with a drama.

"The first session today is called *Masks.* We hope you like it."

Paul began distributing paper plates to his teammates. I was confused. *Are they setting those aside for lunch? The pizza isn't here yet.*

The team stood in a line at the front of the room. Then, one by one, they lifted the plates. Each had a face with a smile drawn on it.

In pairs, the team members stepped up to a set of microphones and acted out a scenario. The first bit was about two people at a party; one offered the other a cigarette. Before responding, the person who'd been offered to smoke took down his mask and told us why he didn't want to smoke. He said his grandparents had died from lung cancer, and he didn't want that to happen to him. He also had no interest in it but felt pressured to partake because of the party atmosphere. After putting his mask back up, he accepted the cigarette, and the scene ended.

Two new people stepped up and began talking about church. One told us she secretly liked praying and going to Mass but didn't want to tell the other for fear she'd be made fun of. I could relate to that. I'd doubted God for a long time after Mary Katherine's death, but I was now convinced He was real and wanted a personal relationship with Him. I hoped to grow in my faith through Confirmation, but it seemed like some people in my class were treating it like a joke or a rite of passage—just something we did as Catholics. Everyone acknowledged the changing of their names, but few seemed to recognize the transformation of their hearts. I longed for a community like this, whose love for the Lord united them, but my fear of people making fun of me or calling me a "Jesus freak" kept me in silence.

The drama ended with a scene about divorce. This last scenario struck me most because it flipped the concept of hiding how you feel on its head. One person's parents were getting a divorce, and the other asked how they were handling it. It was clear the person really cared about how the separation was affecting their friend. My heart soared, thinking the skit would end with a testament to true friendship.

"I'm fine," said the hurting friend, who abruptly changed the subject.

"Okay," the other said slowly.

"Well, if you ever need to talk, I'm here for you."

Waving their compassion away like a fly, the first replied, "I know. Let's go do something! I just need to get out of the house."

Rather than share what was going on in her heart, she sought to push her problems away. What she failed to realize was that she had pushed away her friends in the process. I could relate to that.

~ ~ ~

"Light enters through the wound."

I love this line. I first heard it in the movie adaptation of Madeleine L'Engle's classic work, *A Wrinkle in Time*. I heard a similar phrase not long after that, while on a different retreat. Someone asked the presenters how they would recommend studying the lives of the saints, to which one of them responded, "Meet a saint at the time in their life when they first encountered God's mercy." In other words, find where they messed up big-time and how God used the experience to bring the saint-then-sinner back to Him.

In my mind, saints could do no wrong. For some reason, my picture book didn't delve into the details of St. Francis's fornication or St. Augustine's illegitimate son. People tend to gloss over those and go straight to the founding of the Franciscans or Augustine's dramatic conversion. Rather than exposing the saints-once-sinners, we fast-forward to them performing miracles and seeing visions, but that's not how the stories started. When I'm tempted to cower in a corner instead of share my story, I recall the lives of saints like Francis and Augustine—the real stories, with parts that aren't pretty. Like mine.

I don't know about you, but I don't look back at my middle school self and think, *Wow, she had it all together*. And I can say with certainty that I'd never want to revisit that time in my life. Don't get me wrong, it wasn't all bad, but there were plenty of things that weren't so great. I don't mean petty things like periods or pimples either; I'm talking about the onset of serious addictions.

When I was first introduced to Catherine of Siena, I never imagined we'd have something so shameful in common. I assumed she'd been holy from the time she was in a high chair. I later discovered that Catherine experienced many temptations during her short life, including those against purity. In his book *When God Asks for an Undivided Heart,* Fr. Andrew Apostoli, CFR, wrote about one of these instances in Catherine's life: "A particularly violent and prolonged struggle [against chastity] lasted over a period of two days. When the temptations finally ended, our Lord appeared to her. Catherine asked Him: 'Lord, where were you when I needed you during this trial?' Our Lord answered her: 'Catherine, I was in your heart all along strengthening you!'"

I refused to expose these parts of my heart for years because I thought no one would understand. I thought I was the only one dealing with the things I was keeping locked inside. I thought telling anyone could be a cause for judgment, mockery, and scorn. I didn't know that when light enters our wounds—when we open up about our struggles—we actually begin to heal.

~ ~ ~

I was brought back to reality by the sound of my classmates clapping. The skit had ended, and we were told to break into small groups. I wasn't sure if I wanted to share what was going through my mind.

We talked about the skit and what stood out to us, and our group leader ended our discussion by asking, "Who's the most mask-free person you know?"

I probably said *Jesus.* Honestly, I don't know what I said or what anyone else in my group shared. By that point, I'd drank an entire bottle of water and needed to pee. I was done talking. We had a short break between sessions, so I booked it to the bathroom.

As I was coming out of the stall, I was caught off guard by Rachel. She was washing her hands. She saw me, smiled, and asked, "How are you liking the retreat?"

I didn't think a public restroom was the right place to get deep, so I kept it simple. "It's good."

We switched places, and she began drying her hands with paper towels while I washed mine.

"Are you Morgan?" Rachel's next question surprised me.

We weren't wearing name tags; social media wasn't a thing yet; and as far as I knew, I hadn't committed any crimes that would have warranted my appearance on the news. How did she know my name? She seemed cool, and I trusted her, so I answered slowly.

"Yeah…"

Beaming, Rachel said, "I just want you to know everyone in my small group said you don't wear masks and aren't afraid to be yourself."

She paused, letting the effect of her words sink in. *Me? Mask-free?* I was humbled by my classmates' compliments. I wanted to ask who the people were, but I knew that wasn't the point.

Rachel concluded, "I think that's really cool."

A weak word of thanks was all I could manage before she spun on her heel and headed back to the main room. If only they knew the secrets I'd been hiding for years.

~ ~ ~

My parents aren't perfect. Shocker, I know. They got it from their parents, who got it from their parents, who got it from our first parents, Adam and Eve. Yeah, original sin…I guess you could say that it runs in the family. I know my parents did their best in raising me, and they were and still are amazing, but there were failures on their part that have taken a long time for me to forgive. One was something I know they never intended.

I don't recall my parents really regulating what we watched on TV. When we were still pretty young, they allowed me and my siblings to watch an R-rated movie with them that opened with a graphic sex scene. My senses were overwhelmed by what I saw, and I didn't know how to process it. I felt extremely guilty. I started to watch that scene when I was home alone. When that wasn't enough, I turned to other movies, adult TV shows, and pictures on the internet. Although I'd never heard the term "pornography," I knew I had a problem, and I couldn't stop.

As it does for many people, this addiction led to another serious sin that lasted much longer: masturbation. I don't remember when I stopped looking at porn—it was sometime in middle school—but I will never forget my struggles with masturbation. For a long time, I didn't even know there was a term for it. I just knew I was in darkness and addicted to things beyond my control. I knew I was committing a serious sin and had separated myself from God. I knew I needed help. It wasn't much, but the light of this knowledge was enough to expose the gaping wound in my heart. Much to my surprise, the Lord's tender touch did indeed enter through there.

~ ~ ~

"Hey, guys! I'm Rachel, and today I want to talk to you about chastity."

It was the last talk of the retreat, and none of us were prepared for it. We'd been on a "chastity" retreat earlier in the year, where two older women mainly talked about STDs and the evils of abortion. As much as I liked Rachel, I was afraid of what she would say next.

"I'm sure some of you have heard the term 'chastity' before. Maybe some of you know so much about it you could get up here and give this talk. Maybe some of you have never heard of it. So, I want to start off by explaining what chastity is, and what it's not, so that we're all on the same page. In one word, chastity is respect: respect for yourself, respect for other people, and respect for sex itself. God has created sex for two purposes: bonding and babies. I've never been married, but when you vow to be together through the good *and* the bad, the gift of sex bonds you to help you through those hard times. Sex is so special that I like to think of it as being placed on a pedestal, only to be accessed in marriage, and then to be kept within that marriage."

I liked that analogy. I'd never heard sex described that way. I thought it was beautiful. It also made a lot of sense to me. Up until that point, I saw sex as unholy and inhuman. It made me feel dirty when I saw it on TV or heard it talked about at school. I began to realize my only experience of sex was seeing it through the distorted lenses of pornography and trashy media.

"Chastity is a virtue, which means it's a good habit. It's for everyone, in any vocation; whether you're a priest, a married person, or a teenager, chastity is for you. And it's not about the past. That means if you've seen things you shouldn't have seen(*gulp*) or done things you shouldn't have done(*internal gasp*) you can choose to start living, or reliving, the virtue of chastity *today*. I know it isn't easy, so I'd like to give you my three favorite tips on how to live the virtue of chastity.

"First, be bold. Many people have chosen chastity, but no one really talks about it—at least, not in everyday conversations, like in the hallways at school. And that's okay. Forcing faith-based conversations isn't always the best idea. However, having these conversations with trusted family members, friends, and people you date is absolutely essential to living this virtue. It creates an opportunity for those we love to share their own struggles and perhaps give advice. It also allows healing, as bringing our wounds to the light makes a way for God's mercy to enter our hearts."

~ ~ ~

"Mom?"

"Yeah, babe?"

"Can I talk to you about something?"

"Sure. What's up?"

My mom is a very nonchalant person. Sometimes her casual demeanor frustrates me when I'd like her to take a situation more seriously. However, I have to admit that it's been my saving grace, as it has made starting conversations like this a lot easier.

"I don't really know how to say it…," I began.

I couldn't look her in the eyes. What if she never saw me the same way? I wondered what was running through her mind. We'd covered the big bases before: Santa wasn't real, you had to have sex to have a baby. But this, I thought, was a conversation no mother and daughter should have to have. My mom, sensing my trepidation, didn't push it.

"That's okay," she said.

When I still hesitated, she added, "You know you can tell me anything, and no matter what, I will always love you."

That was all I needed to hear. I started bawling. I told her everything: about the movie we'd watched and how it made me feel, how I'd been looking up pictures and disrespecting my body ever since, and how I couldn't stop. My mom listened as I poured my heart out, and when I was finished, she didn't look at me differently; she didn't call me dirty; and she didn't say she was disappointed in me. Instead, she held me as I wept and assured me I was not alone in my struggles.

"It's pretty common for kids to start dealing with this stuff during puberty," she told me.

Her words spoke healing and comfort, which were balm on my wounds. When I eventually confided in close friends, I was surprised to learn that my mom was right. Many of them were also struggling with sexual sins. This openness and honesty strengthened our friendships and allowed us to become a support group for one another— much like Rachel said it would. Now I had people both in heaven and on earth praying for me. It was a welcome relief to know I wasn't alone.

After confiding in close family members and friends, I knew there was someone else I needed to turn to in my addiction: my Father in heaven. I was terrified to say the words "pornography" and "masturbation" in a confessional, but I was convinced it was what I needed to be healed. The Holy Spirit, who'd been strengthened in me at the confirmation, gave me the courage I needed. I'll admit, confessing my sins to a priest was awful the first time, even if I was behind a screen; my stomach felt like it was in knots the entire time. I wondered if it would be a sin to puke on the priest. Saying one simple sentence—"I have given into the sins of pornography and masturbation more times than I can count"—was torture. I felt so ashamed and so far from God. All I could see was my sin. I wept bitterly, wondering what words the priest would use to condemn me. *Does he have the power to send me to hell?* I felt like a criminal whose fate would be determined by whatever words were spoken next.

After what felt like an eternity, I heard the priest speak. For the first time, I felt the presence of God the Father in the confessional;

though the screen, crucifix, and priest remained the same, a light broke through the darkness inside me. The weight I'd been carrying for so long began to lighten. It felt like someone was taking the burden off me and placing it on themselves instead. I looked at the crucifix, fresh tears streaming down my face. I understood that the Father had taken the weight of my sin and placed it on His Son, who destroyed death so that I could have a life. I had entered into this life through baptism, but it was through my confirmation that He brought me back to Him.

"I absolve you from your sins in the name of the Father, and of the Son, and of the Holy Spirit."

Though I didn't understand the reality of sacramental grace at the time, it didn't prevent me from experiencing the fullness of its effects. I went forth from that confessional completely transformed; I was forgiven and free. Just like the saints I'd read about all my life, I hadn't been abandoned by God when I was most in need of His mercy. Rather, in my darkest hour, the Lord remained present in my heart, strengthening me when I felt most alone. He placed people in my life to lead me back to Him. Even if I haven't lived this virtue perfectly, choosing chastity on that retreat had a profound impact on my life and my relationships—especially the romantic ones.

~ ~ ~

"My second tip," Rachel said, "is to be prepared. When you start to date, have a plan for your dates. Don't get caught in the 'hanging out' trap, where all you do is watch movies in your parents' basement. Whether the lights are on or off, you're more likely to be tempted against chastity in that situation than you would be in a restaurant. Just saying. So, plan your dates! Do fun activities in public places, and include other people.

"Being prepared also means knowing your boundaries," Rachel continued.

"This includes physical boundaries—because sex is physical, duh—but it also involves spiritual and emotional boundaries. I know a lot of people who've given parts of their minds, hearts, and bodies away because they feel pressured to do so by their partners, who still end up leaving them. It's impossible to plan what to say or do in every situation, but setting boundaries in advance will help you choose chastity more readily when you're faced with temptation.

"Finally, be not afraid. If something doesn't feel right, it probably isn't. Don't be afraid to get out of a situation or away from a certain person. One bad decision isn't worth spending an eternity separated from God. Don't be afraid to stand up for your friends and for yourself. It's better to be made fun of for staying on the straight and narrow than to wind up suffering forever because you chose to follow the crowd."

I wish I had taken that last piece of advice.

THE PRODIGAL DAUGHTER

"So…do you wanna be my girlfriend?"

Never mind that we'd been texting on and off for six months before he even asked me on a date. This guy—a junior from a school down south—was asking me to be his girlfriend, and I was over-the-moon excited about it. I was a sophomore in high school, and the dating scene was entirely new to me. How old was Taylor Swift in that one song? It didn't matter; *I* was fifteen and felt like I'd found true love.

After my eighth-grade retreat, it was important to me that anyone I dated respect me—my body and my beliefs. I didn't think I had anything to worry about with this guy. He was super sweet and seemed to be into his faith. One of the first times I saw him, he was wearing a T-shirt that read, REAL MEN LOVE JESUS. That had to be legit, right?

It quickly became clear that we weren't "the ones" for each other. He was into computers and techy stuff, and I wasn't. He liked the party scene, and I didn't. We lived half an hour apart, which was a lot since we went to different schools. In less time than we'd been "talking" before our relationship, we broke up. Even though he ended things, I wasn't upset. I knew it was for the best. Besides, most of our dates were spent making out in our parents' basements—the kind of thing Rachel had warned us against. But no one—not even her—had told me how far was "too far."

Less than a month later, I started dating a different guy. I was a junior now, and he was a senior. We were in love. I don't know how else to explain it. We'd been friends for years, but over time, our friendship naturally developed into a beautiful relationship. I enjoyed every minute I spent with him, and we were pretty much together 24/7. I never imagined someone could make me so happy or care about me so deeply.

My boyfriend and I often talked about a future together. His ideal career was one our hometown didn't offer—so we brainstormed where we would live. We threw out several ideas before settling on Chicago. I would find myself fantasizing about a family in the "Windy City," but it didn't matter if it was Illinois or Iceland. I would have followed that boy anywhere. This proved to be my downfall.

One night, as my boyfriend and I were making out next to my car, I felt his hand go to my butt. He'd never touched me that way before, and I didn't like it. I stopped and pulled away from him.

"What's wrong?" he asked, confused.

You touched my butt. That's what's wrong! I thought. But that's not what I said. I didn't say anything for a long time.

I felt frozen. I knew I hadn't liked it when he touched me, but I couldn't articulate why. It just seemed like something we shouldn't do. I wish Rachel had ended her talk with a chastity checklist. "Don't have sex" was a given, but no one ever said, "Also, don't let him touch your butt," or "Don't let him touch your boobs." All I'd been told was, "You have to decide how far 'too far' is for you." That was awful advice, but I didn't know it. Hence, my moral dilemma.

How could my boyfriend treat me like this? Doesn't he love me? I'm fine with making out, but I don't want to go further. No one said it was wrong, though…maybe it's just me? What if this is what people do when they're in love? My last boyfriend never did this, but maybe it's because we weren't serious. Is this what serious looks like? We're not having sex…I told him I'm saving myself for marriage, and he says he wants to wait too. I trust him; he loves me. If sex is "too far," maybe we can do whatever else we want?

For the *Harry Potter* fans out there, I want you to picture the scene from the first movie where Harry is taunted by Lord Voldemort.

Harry is promised that, if he hands over the sorcerer's stone, his parents will be brought back to life. Deep down, Harry knows this isn't true but is tempted because his desire is so strong. That night, by my car, the devil was testing me in a similar way.

This isn't a big deal, came a voice in my mind.

Your boyfriend loves you. If he would do this, it must be a loving action. You already know you're going to get married, so why not enjoy each other now? Doing this will bring you closer as a couple. Your relationship will be stronger than ever.

"You Liar!" Though these were the words Harry screamed at Voldemort, they were not the words I used that night. Unlike Harry, I didn't defend what I knew to be true. Instead, I gave into the wiles of the devil, who led me to believe that the further I went with my boyfriend, the more "in love" we would be. But Satan lied to me. The further my boyfriend and I went, the more out of love and into lust we fell. We became addicted to our sexual sins. Suddenly, our relationship wasn't about enjoying each other's company. It was about finding time to be alone. Though we were doing things that brought us closer physically, our hearts couldn't have been further apart.

Once, after an intense dry-humping session, my boyfriend told me he'd be right back. I'd stopped responding, as I'd already reached climax (another sexual term I didn't understand at the time). With an embarrassed look on his face, he explained he had to go "finish." Only later did I realize his implication was masturbation. When the ugly truth dawned on me, I was devastated. I knew masturbation was wrong but had no idea how to navigate these boundaries in the context of a romantic relationship. I felt utterly powerless to make a change after we'd messed up so many times and felt deeply ashamed for treating my boyfriend this way—and myself. Why had no one told me about these things? Surely other people were struggling. Why was no one saying anything?

I was also unaware of how risky kissing with the tongue was, which I considered "making out." I'd heard some people say that, prior to marriage, physical stuff outside sex wasn't a big deal. The best explanation I've heard since then for why this is *not* the case comes from the chastity educator, Christopher West. In his book

Good News About Sex and Marriage, West addresses "lines" in romantic relationships (i.e., physical boundaries). He begins by noting that "before the line is drawn along the scale of physical behaviors, it must be drawn in the human heart." Well, it's pretty hard to think with your head and heart when your hormones are racing. Now I knew what Rachel had meant when she told us, "Be prepared." After highlighting lines in the heart, West names explicit physical boundaries for premarital relationships:

> Physical behaviors that aim to arouse the body in preparation for intercourse (fondling each other's genitals or breasts, and even some kinds of extended kissing and embracing) are not appropriate expressions of affection for the unmarried. When there is simply no moral possibility of consummated love [i.e., sex in marriage], it is, in fact, unloving to arouse someone to the point of physical craving for intercourse. If either the man or woman is brought to the verge of climax, or has reached climax, or is aroused to the point of being tempted to masturbate, such a couple 'crossed the line' *a long time before* and is in serious need of examining their hearts and their motives. (West, Ch. 4, 76)

Although I wasn't being tempted to masturbate by the things we were doing, my boyfriend was, and it was wrong for me to arouse him to that point. With every sinful act, my heart was being torn apart until—finally—it shattered into a million pieces. Thankfully, God can work with broken parts.

~ ~ ~

I'm sure you've heard the phrase, "Breakups suck," more than once in your life. However, I'm here to argue that—while parts of them certainly do—they are overall a good thing. A *holy* thing. A *virtuous* thing. Why? Because they are the product of growing up and growing in maturity. Being able to break up, if needed, shows that a couple can discern when they are no longer best for each other. In this situation, a couple can show more love for one another by breaking up than by staying in an unhealthy relationship.

Breaking up can even be likened to loving as Christ does. In the Gospel of John, Jesus tells His disciples, "This is my commandment, that you love one another as I have loved you. Greater love has no man than this, that a man lay down his life for his friends" (15:12–13). Some people break up for selfish reasons, but when a breakup occurs out of willingness for the good of another, it is the kind of sacrificial love Christ refers to here. For me and my boyfriend, breaking up was what we needed to grow in maturity and purity. A word of advice: if you're struggling to remain chaste but know you need to break up, do it over the phone. This way, you can't be tempted to get physical in person.

It was early evening, and I was at my grandparents' house. I have no idea why—it was weird. I had the house to myself, and I spent the half hour leading up to the phone call writing a prayer on an old piece of notepaper. Fighting back tears, I begged God to give me the grace to do what needed to be done. I couldn't believe that less than a year before, we'd been dancing at homecoming. Our love had been so sweet, so innocent, and so pure. What the hell happened?

We'd broken up before, after about five months. The reason? We couldn't control ourselves. I'd started crying on most of our "dates" because my conscience kept nagging at me. I could tell my boyfriend hated seeing me miserable and was genuinely trying to respect me. We would set boundaries and resolve not to cross them again. But it never worked. By that time, we were the blind leading the blind. Unable to get a hold on our addictions, we broke up sometime in March of my junior year.

I was depressed for weeks afterward, as was he. The classes we shared became torture. In the hallways, we avoided eye contact. People could see how much we were hurting, and I was terrified they would find out why. I'd never been a partyer, a drinker, or a drug user. What would people say if they found out I was much worse? I felt like everyone was whispering about me. Did they know how far we had gone?

Prom was impending, and the thought of not going together was excruciating. So, we did what most high school couples do after breaking up: we got back together. I learned later that acts of intimacy bond a couple on emotional and hormonal levels, which makes breaking up difficult, even impossible. I knew sex had that effect, so it made sense that other physical stuff would do the same. I thought I was missing my boyfriend, but what I was actually missing were the sensations he aroused in me. Therefore, when we got back together, the nature of our relationship remained the same. We continued to use each other, seeking pleasure in place of the person. Prom night was no different.

I'd been so wrapped up in preparations for the day that I hadn't given any thought to sleeping arrangements. We'd just gotten to the dance, and a slow song was playing. My boyfriend took me by the hand and led me onto the dance floor. Pulling me close so only I could hear him, he whispered, "I reserved a room for us at the cabin."

I was taken aback. I knew we wouldn't have sex, but still, sleeping together was sleeping together. I assumed this was something we'd never do, so I never addressed it. I knew we were staying with his friends at a cabin somewhere, but where we'd all sleep hadn't been on my radar.

My thoughts became jumbled. I went from confused to submissive to excited in a matter of seconds. I hadn't chosen chastity in months, so why fight anymore? I'd given the devil a stronghold in my heart long ago, and he was all too eager to continue leading me along the open road to destruction.

"Can't wait," I whispered back, the suggestive lyrics playing around us, serving to further dull my senses.

I didn't recognize myself anymore. When my last boyfriend took me to prom, I hadn't even gone to the after-party with him. Now I would be sharing a bed with my boyfriend. What a difference one year and one bad decision could make. Even though we didn't have sex that night, we did things that I'm sure sounded like it. I wondered what the others thought of us. I wondered if any of them were having sex. I pushed the dark thoughts away, telling myself that what we were doing was love. What anyone else thought was on them.

~ ~ ~

"Did you hear that?"

My boyfriend was home from college for the weekend. It was early September, my senior year, and we were as caught up in lust as ever. We'd spent most of Sunday together, but as he was getting ready to leave, we started making out next to his car. Things quickly escalated until we were aggressively fondling each other. I thought we were alone when I heard the backdoor open. My stomach dropped. Who was there?

My dad had caught us a few weeks before. I'd broken my curfew, which was unfortunately becoming the norm for me. That time, it was because my boyfriend and I stayed after work to spend some "alone time" in my car. What we thought would be a few minutes may have turned into a few hours had my dad not come to find me. At first, we weren't sure who the person driving around and honking at us was. It was dark, and we'd fogged up the windows. I was scared and startled by the intruder, especially since I was shirtless. When I realized it was my father, I felt a shame unlike anything I'd ever known. You'd think I'd have learned my lesson that night, but no— it took one final blow to force me to see the big picture.

I stopped to see who it was but didn't see anyone in the garage. Had whoever it was gone back inside? *It's fine,* came an all-too-familiar whisper. I couldn't tell if the devil or my boyfriend had said it, and at that point, I didn't care. I seemed incapable of making a good decision or seeing the light. I'd become a slave to sensuality. Content to continue our caressing, I pushed my conscience away. I never looked back, which is why I never saw the next breakup coming.

As it turned out, it was my eleven-year-old sister who saw us. She'd opted to stay home that day while my dad went to the farm and my mom took Seth to practice. Confused and crying, Erin had called Mom, who confronted me later. It was the rude awakening I needed, but I didn't want to see it. I'd managed to compromise my morals and talk down my conscience for months. I couldn't fathom a life where lust wasn't at the forefront.

I thought I would drown in depression. I felt like I hadn't just hit rock bottom but was trapped there, forced to face my unspeakable sins every time I looked at my sister. I didn't know how to begin to say sorry to all those I had hurt and disappointed.

I begged God to help me make the call I knew was going to be so painful. I begged Him for the grace of a good conversation. I prayed for healing for me and my boyfriend. I prayed for wisdom and strength. I prayed my boyfriend would not only understand but also agree with me about the need to break up. I clutched the paper close to my heart as I picked up the phone.

At first, my boyfriend was angry. He was angry at himself for hurting me and angry at the situation with my sister. I think it was his way of dealing with the shame. I understood, as shame was something I was also coming to terms with. I think he may have felt helpless, too, forced to have such a hard conversation over the phone. I hated how I was hurting him—how I had hurt him for so long—and told him so. We both cried and apologized for the ways we'd failed. The tears were healing and brought a wave of peace to each of us. The finality of our decision was daunting, but it was the best decision we'd made in a long time.

Though my boyfriend and I broke up on good terms, I was left with many mental and emotional scars from the sins we'd committed. In addition, my addiction to masturbation—which I thought was gone for good—returned with a vengeance. I've been told this is normal after a long period of sexual stimulation, but that didn't make me feel better. If anything, it reminded me of the countless regrets I had about the relationship. I spent most of my senior year in a deep darkness. I refused to tell anyone how I was feeling and felt like things would never get better. The light had gone out of my life, and I was the one who'd shown Him the door.

THE NOT-SO-GOOD SHEPHERD

My freshman year of college was far from the best time of my life. I was still somewhat fresh out of a breakup and battling an addiction to masturbation that had resurfaced as a result. Not to mention that I had plenty of other stressors during my transition from high school to college: moving out of state, leaving behind loved ones, and being undecided on a major. I didn't have a clue what I wanted to do with my life, let alone what God had in store for it.

Everyone seemed determined to fit me into a mold. If I'd received a dollar for every time someone asked, "What do you want to do, Morgan?" I could have paid for college two times over. (And Catholic college isn't cheap.) It was agonizing. I knew they were all trying to help me, but I felt worthless for not wanting to be a teacher, a nurse, or whatever else was held out to me. I berated myself for not knowing what I wanted to do for the next…ever. I listened to lies that told me I wasn't good enough, that I would never amount to anything, and that I would never figure it out. Little did I know that the lost sheep are the Lord's favorites.

~ ~ ~

It was miserably hot that day in the Holy Land. It was May 2018, and I was on a pilgrimage—a college graduation present. However, I wasn't feeling very grateful for it at the moment. I'd graduated on a Saturday, driven all my belongings home on Sunday, and boarded a plane for Tel Aviv early Monday morning. We'd bounced around Israel for over a week, finally landing in Jerusalem. I was exhausted. Our itinerary broke down each day by the hour. I felt like I was drinking from a spiritual fire hose, and I couldn't take it anymore.

I was relieved when our tour bus pulled up to a church I'd never heard of—Dominus Flevit. Maybe I'd finally get some peace and quiet. That's when our chaplain announced we would be having Mass there shortly. *Dang it,* I thought. *Don't these people know how to rest? What's so special about this place, anyway?* So far, I had understood the significance of every place we'd visited: the mountain where Elijah heard God's still small voice; the cave where the angel Gabriel announced to Mary that she was to be the Mother of God; and the tomb where Jesus resurrected from the dead. Crazy stuff. What could top that?

Translated from Latin, *Dominus Flevit* means "The Lord wept" and refers to the site where Jesus prophesied the destruction of Jerusalem. Inside the church, there's a window directly behind the altar that overlooks the ancient city, inviting viewers to enter into the mystery. I'd never given much thought to this passage. However, I will never forget the homily from our Mass there.

Approaching the pulpit, Father paused and looked back at the scene that lay before us. It was quite picturesque. The sun was shining, and the sounds of the city seemed far away. No one sensed impending doom.

Turning back to us with a glint in his eye, Father asked, "You know the image of a shepherd holding a lamb across his shoulders? Well, did you know that the only way the shepherd is able to carry the sheep is by breaking its leg?"

He must have seen an array of astonished expressions, because Father chuckled and continued, "When a sheep strays from the flock, it acts in disobedience to the shepherd, who knows what's best for the sheep. When the shepherd seeks it out, the sheep might not realize it has strayed and refuse to return. A shepherd can't carry a stubborn sheep. Imagine the fight it would put up. So, what does the shepherd do? He breaks its leg."

~ ~ ~

It didn't take me long to gravitate to a group of cute guys the second week of college. Shortly after we were introduced, they invited me to go longboarding. Never mind that I didn't know what longboarding was. I jumped on the opportunity—literally.

"So how does this work?"

The guy closest to me laughed, though not unkindly.

He answered, "Push off with one foot, and once you're coasting, put the foot you pushed off with behind the other."

That didn't seem so hard.

"Okay. How do you stop?"

He seemed stumped. After a beat, he shrugged and said, "You just kind of jump off."

~ ~ ~

"Only after the shepherd breaks its leg does the sheep realize its complete dependence on the shepherd and yield to being carried. After such a traumatic experience, the sheep will never stray again."

~ ~ ~

"Morgan, slow down!"

"You're going too fast!"

"Jump!"

"LOOK OUT!"

Sometimes, it really sucks to be a sheep.

~ ~ ~

"The shepherd finds no joy in breaking the leg of the sheep," Father said solemnly.

"I imagine it causes him as much pain to inflict the injury as it does for the sheep to experience it. I picture the shepherd's eyes welling up with tears, sorry for the sheep having strayed and sorry that this was the only way to win it back. I see him lifting the sheep carefully onto his shoulders, speaking softly to soothe it. Safe at last in the arms of the shepherd, the two return home. Once there, the shepherd tends to the wounds of his sheep, always exercising great tenderness. Over time, the sheep is restored to full health—never to stray again."

~ ~ ~

"Are you okay?"

"You guys, she's bleeding!"

"Look at her ankle! Is it coming through the skin?"

"Where are we? We have to call an ambulance!"

While I loved biking and rollerblading, putting two feet on the same contraption was a foreign concept to me. My brother had a skateboard when we were kids, but I'd never gone near it. We didn't live near an ocean or the mountains, so I'd never surfed or snowboarded. In short, I had no idea what I was doing; the lightning-fast intro session hadn't helped either.

The four guys ran over to me, panic lining their faces. One called an ambulance and ran to find a street sign to lead them to our location. Another put his arm around me, propping me up into a sitting position. A third called other friends, asking them to meet us at the hospital. The fourth rooted through his bag and offered me whatever he could find. Since my brain was struggling to make sense of the situation, it fixed on one thing—that I was an idiot for letting this happen. I began apologizing profusely.

"I am so sorry, you guys! This is the worst. I'm so sorry! I didn't mean to mess everything up. I'm so sorry!"

They exchanged bewildered looks, wondering what the crazy girl was going on about. Finally, one of them cut me off.

"Morgan, it's not your fault. You have nothing to be sorry for."

Almost as an afterthought, he added, "Also, you can cry now!"

I'd been talking nonstop. Suddenly, my brain was forced to process the disturbing sight of my ankle and the intense pain firing up my left leg. The bone wasn't coming through the skin, but it was close. My ankle was sideways, and the section that had scraped against the pavement was bleeding. It looked as bad as it felt. I didn't know if I would pass out, throw up, or do both. I'd never broken a bone, and now—as I found out later—I'd broken two at once.

I was taken aback when one of them asked, "Morgan, can we pray over you?"

I wasn't sure what shocked me more—the fact that I had just obliterated my ankle or that a random guy was offering to pray with me. Stunned, I nodded.

The four bowed their heads, closed their eyes, and made the sign of the cross. Each man prayed from his heart, asking God to be with me and heal me. I had never been prayed for in such a profound, personal way—that itself was a healing experience. In the midst of my suffering, I sensed the Lord holding me through those young men's prayers. As one of them handed me a crucifix to hold onto, I was sure of it. Everything was going to be okay.

~ ~ ~

"When we're humbled, there is a temptation toward bitterness. We might ask, 'Lord, why would You let this happen to me? To my friend? To my family?' We often question what we do not understand. It is only when we admit our weaknesses and own up to how we've wandered that we can see why God allowed this to happen: to bring us back to Him."

~ ~ ~

I was very tempted toward bitterness when I broke my ankle. I knew God was using this experience to show me that I had a community I could lean on and learn from, but I remained guarded. I was in desperate need of healing, and not just for my ankle. While that wound was visible to everyone, I kept my sexual scars hidden. But that didn't keep them from haunting me.

I believed breaking up with my boyfriend would solve all my problems. I thought peace, purity, and clarity would descend like a cloud and transfigure me into a new person overnight. I thought my countless confessions would cleanse me of the guilt and shame I couldn't seem to get past. I thought life would go back to "normal," that I could overcome all adversity on my own, and that I'd be happy again in the blink of an eye. I was wrong.

At a loss for how to properly channel my emotional turmoil, I turned to overeating. Instead of the "freshman 15," I gained over twenty pounds that year. I despised my body and blamed myself for all the evil that had befallen me, including my broken ankle. My inner demons seemed to be manifesting themselves from the inside out, and I was terrified someone would see through my "I'm fine" facade.

I tried to fly under the radar. I was suffering from a lack of motivation and had the grades to prove it. I hoped to blend in with other apathetic freshmen, but having a broken ankle didn't exactly allow for that. All my professors went out of their way to talk to me; one in particular often talked to me about potential career paths.

"You mentioned you haven't declared a major. I can tell you're an avid listener, and from what you've shared in class, you seem to want to help people. It got me thinking you might make a good counselor. Have you been to counseling before?" I replied that I hadn't. I didn't add that it was because I didn't think I needed it.

"You should consider making an appointment with one of the counselors on campus," my professor suggested. "The services for students are free, and it would give you an idea as to whether you'd like to pursue a degree in psychology." Curious, I agreed to look into it.

When I arrived at the clinic a few weeks later, I felt like I was stepping into a doctor's office. The waiting room was small, and everyone looked uncomfortable. When I walked up to the receptionist, she smiled and handed me a clipboard with a set of forms to fill out. Assuming it was a standard health assessment, I groaned inwardly as I made my way to a vacant seat. I'd just been released from crutches and could walk on my left foot again with little to no pain. *Guess I have to count the blessings.*

When I flipped open the chart, I was surprised to see several pages composed of nonmedical questions. These items included whether I experienced body-shaming, broken relationships, or anxiety surrounding food or eating. I was prompted to check the boxes that applied to me. I was stunned by how many did. I marked those three, as well as a handful of others, but couldn't bring myself to address my addiction to masturbation. I'd come face-to-face with my physical frailty when I broke my ankle, but refused to admit my weakness when it came to sexual sins.

After a significant wait, I was directed to a door on the left side of the room. When the first words out of the counselor's mouth were, "How are you feeling today?" I thought I might lose it. *This is ridiculous.* I took a deep breath before answering. *I'm just here to ask about her job.*

"Fine," I offered.

The counselor looked over my form before returning her attention to me.

"What brings you in here today?" she chirped.

Yep. Definitely feels like a doctor's office.

"I'm not sure what I want to do as a career, and one of my professors suggested that I look into counseling. I thought I'd try it out to see if it would be something I might like to do."

Her smile was replaced by a furrowed brow. I guess she'd never gotten that answer before.

"Okay," she said slowly.

"Well, since you're here, I'd like to ask about a few things you marked on your list. Would that be all right? And we can go from there."

Begrudgingly, I nodded. *Let's get this over with.*

~ ~ ~

I didn't see how I could overcome the addiction this time. I believed I'd beaten it once and for all in middle school. But seven years later, I was still struggling. Though I'd confided in family and friends when I was younger, that seemed out of the question. I couldn't even muster the courage to share this with a stranger. After all, I was older. I was in college. I was a woman! *It makes sense for a girl during puberty or for a man anytime in his life, but not for me now. I'm the only one,* I thought. *I am alone in this.*

These lies beat against the walls of my mind like a brass drum. I loved the friends I was making and wanted to trust them, but for all that, I remained in isolation for the first part of college. Even counseling didn't seem to help. I opened up about some things there, including my relationships, and worked through my disordered eating, but my sexual sins were more deeply rooted. The shame they brought to the surface scared me, to the point where I stopped believing I would or could ever break free.

6

LEAD OF LOVE

I reached a breaking point on the eve of my twenty-first birthday. I'd gotten home from school the week before and was still messing up. Wearily, I called my parish center to schedule a confession for the following day. I hung up, feeling utterly hopeless. I threw the phone aside and began to despair when I heard a notification bell ding. Fearing I'd broken my phone, I picked it up to inspect the damage. No cracked screen, just a random text from a friend I hadn't seen in a while. She said she knew I was turning twenty-one and wanted to help me celebrate such a significant milestone. I was tempted to tell her I wasn't feeling up to it, but something inside me said, *Invite her over.* Maybe God had something in mind for the occasion.

We spent the first half of the night catching up and watching a few episodes of our favorite show. As time went on, my mind turned to masturbation. It had gotten to the point where it was all I could think about. It made it impossible to enjoy anything because I was always afraid of when I would mess up again. I knew it had become too heavy of a burden to carry alone, but I was afraid my friend would judge me.

I began to have flashbacks of middle school. I could see my mom as we sat together in the living room—the first person I'd ever told. She hadn't shamed me, nor had any of my friends after her. Instead, they rallied around me, prayed for me, and praised God for my deliverance. *It's true that God delivered me once,* I thought, *but He shouldn't have to do it again.* I wrongly believed the resurgence of my addiction was a penance of sorts, a just punishment for a sinner like me. I inwardly vowed not to share that I was struggling again with anyone. It was too risky.

Satan agreed. *How could you let this happen? You knew better than to let your boyfriend treat you like that. You lived in sin for so long. Your mom tried to tell you it wasn't a good relationship, and your friends tried to warn you, but you wouldn't listen. Now you're broken beyond repair and have no one to blame but yourself. You deserve this.*

I now recognize the voice of the enemy, but I couldn't discern so clearly between spirits that night. Part of what this voice said was true: I *had* known better than to let myself be disrespected and to disrespect the young men I dated. I *had* lived in sin for so long, and the people who loved and cared for me most *had* encouraged me to make better decisions. However, the lies were that I was broken beyond repair, that I deserved to remain in the darkness, and that I was alone.

Tell her, came another voice. The whisper of the Holy Spirit poured forth like soft, soothing rain onto my aching heart. Afraid I would lose my resolve if I didn't act immediately, I turned to my friend.

"Can I talk to you about something?"

"Of course. You know I'm always here for you."

I told her everything: how I'd been exposed to porn when I was little; how that addiction led to a more prolonged struggle with masturbation; how I'd sinned in past relationships, failing to uphold my dignity and that of my boyfriends. I sobbed as I shared how my addiction to masturbation had returned and how I feared it would never go away. When I was finished, she said two words that would change the trajectory of my life forever: "Me too."

I was overwhelmed by the goodness of God. I thought I was beyond His mercy, like the sheep even the shepherd couldn't find, but here He was in the midst of us. He'd sought me in my wanderings and found me through a friend. He provided a way out—one I never expected but for which I will always be grateful.

"Really?" I asked in disbelief.

She nodded. "Yeah. I struggled with it for a long time, not knowing what it was and feeling like I was the only one. I've only told one other person, who's now my accountability partner. I would love to be that person for you too, if that's something you think would be helpful."

Fresh tears surfaced. "That would be really great." I gave her a huge hug, and she held me as I cried some more. I was finally starting to understand what St. Paul meant when he said, *"Rejoice with those who rejoice; weep with those who weep"* (Rom 12:15–18 RSVCE).

~ ~ ~

Less than a month later, I began working at a Catholic summer camp. We were told we'd have one week of staff training, followed by two middle school sessions and one week for high schoolers. Many of the high school students were volunteering at the middle school sessions, which meant they'd be present for staff training. One of those days was dedicated to sharing "testimonies," tales of how we'd each encountered Jesus personally and how He'd changed our lives, etc. I wasn't sure what to include in mine, but since we'd mostly be ministering to middle schoolers, I decided to make a list of things I was dealing with during that time. When I was finished, my list looked something like this:

Mary Katherine dying
Starting my period
Getting braces
Bad acne
Major crushes
Struggling with my looks
Porn and masturbation

Clearly, I had some pretty traumatic experiences in middle school, while others were more common. Seeking to narrow my scope, I asked God what I should share. As I prayed, I was convicted to speak out about my sexual sins. Though fear started to creep back into my heart, I wrote the talk in obedience. *Maybe we'll run out of time so I won't have to share?*

Later that afternoon, the male staff members were directed to one location while we women were ushered into the chapel. There, we were invited to take turns sharing our testimonies in front of the group. Scanning the room, I counted at least thirty women. I started to squirm in my seat. *What if I didn't hear You right, God?* I watched as several women, both young and old, stood up and volunteered their stories. No one was disclosing anything so sensitive or personal.

I thought about the prophet Jonah. He knew God was calling him to preach repentance to the city of Nineveh but was afraid of people's reactions. So he boarded a boat headed in the opposite direction. I didn't want to end up in the belly of a whale, but I didn't want to share my testimony either. Torn, I turned to prayer again. *Jesus, thank You for choosing our group to be the one in the chapel. I know You're here with me, but I'm so afraid. What should I do?* One after another, women continued to share how they'd come closer to God, but none seemed to need His mercy as badly as me.

"A sword will pierce through your own soul, that thoughts out of many hearts may be revealed." This passage from the Gospel of Luke popped into my mind. *Why is God bringing it up now?* Trying to be discreet, I inched my Bible closer and flipped through the thin pages until I came upon Luke 2:35. Since I was majoring in theology, this Bible was one of my textbooks. It was full of insights from various classes in addition to my own highlighted notes. I wasn't sure which source had inspired it, but in giant letters at the bottom right, I'd written, "When I trust You, I don't need to understand."

There it was, plain as day. I had my mission. Peace flooded my heart, dispelling any trace of doubt. I'd lived in fear for too long; it was time to step out of the boat. My vision cleared as a sense of purpose was placed before me. So I took the leap. I boldly stepped forward when it came to my turn. I don't remember what I said, but I felt a spark ignite inside me. I knew the Holy Spirit was inspiring my words. They flowed freely and powerfully, like water bursting forth from behind a dam. When I sat down, I experienced a sense of triumph, like a soldier who'd just slayed an enemy in battle. *Was this how David felt when he defeated Goliath?*

I never could have imagined the impact my story would have. It felt like a bolt of lightning had gone through the room and pierced the heart of every woman present. After I shared, many began their testimonies by saying things like "This isn't what I wrote, but after hearing Morgan speak, I want to share this…" One high school girl confessed through broken sobs that she'd sent pictures of her undergarments to a young man who pressured her to do so. Another confided that she and her boyfriend struggled with dry-humping and had broken up because of it. Emboldened by those around her, one young woman was given the grace to share that she was sexually abused by her brother's best friend when she was a child. This horrific sexual encounter had manifested itself in an addiction to masturbation, which she had been dealing with ever since.

God heard His daughters cry out and came to our rescue. Tears streamed forth as my sisters in Christ experienced this newfound freedom and forgiveness. Many resolved to run to our Lord in the sacrament of reconciliation, some for the first time. When I shared my story with the campers in the weeks that followed, I had dozens of young girls, teenagers, and even adult volunteers approach me, all saying the same thing my friend had: "Me too." I never imagined my testimony would have such a tangible impact; it was an incredibly humbling experience.

Though I'd spoken at hundreds of retreats since Confirmation, no other subject I spoke about seemed to strike people so profoundly. I longed to travel the world, speaking about the freedom I'd found in Christ. I probably would have, too, except for one problem: I had no idea where to start. Unable to reconcile my heart's desire with how I'd make money, find housing, and acquire other necessities for living, I felt like I had no choice but to return to school the following semester. I had to trust that it was where the Lord was leading me.

~ ~ ~

I had first fallen in love with the Lord when I was in eighth grade. I attributed this to the retreats I attended in preparation for Confirmation as well as the influence of a local youth group. This was a game changer for me as I encountered young people from my community who were on fire for God. While all the peers I met there inspired me, one who stood out was Toni.

Toni was several years older than me, and we met the year she came home from college. She wasn't back for a break or because she had graduated either. She dropped out of school to join a religious order. Yeah, you read that right—girl was dropping out of college to become a NUN. And she wasn't even thirty!

I assumed being old and decrepit were prerequisites for such a state in life. I couldn't imagine being called to give my life to God in such a radical way, especially without really "living" first. I had many talks with Toni that summer, and her heart for God transformed my perception of what it truly means to live. I would see her in adoration, kneeling in front of our Lord in the Blessed Sacrament. She was willing to give her whole life to Him, and it was clear that the decision brought her great peace and joy. I wanted to experience that kind of love for the Lord.

I started to wonder if I could best share my story by becoming a sister. After all, sisters were the speakers at many conferences I attended throughout college. I'd also had several friends mention the religious life to me, as had certain priests and mentors. This led me to spend almost every fall and spring break at a different convent. I met with a spiritual director every month. I read every book I could on discernment. I believed this was my calling and was willing to go to the ends of the earth to spread the Good News, if only God would show me the way.

He made it clear to me a year after graduation that this was not the vocation He had in mind for me. I was visiting a convent (of all places), one I had been to many times before. I had never felt drawn to enter this order but always enjoyed visiting and had many friends there.

That evening, they showed a short film called *For Love Alone,* a sixteen-minute documentary of sorts that shows what being a religious sister is all about. I had seen the video many times before, but this night was different. This time, one line struck me so deeply that

I could not deny that the Holy Spirit was speaking to me; in fact, He was calling me out.

"If being a wife and mother isn't at all attractive to you, then you probably wouldn't make a good sister," one nun said into the camera.

I had always wanted to be married. From the time I was little, I'd fantasized about meeting the man of my dreams and sailing off into the sunset; it was how I always saw the story ending. But after making so many mistakes, I was convinced there would be no silver lining to my story. I realized I was drawn to religious life partly because I was running away from marriage. I was afraid of being hurt again. Yet I had become so bogged down by my fears and obsessed with figuring out how to serve God that I'd forgotten about Him altogether.

The still small voice that was growing stronger in my life said two new words that night: "Let go." It seemed like the Lord was inviting me to let go of religious life so that He could hold me instead. I was filled with a deep sense of peace and hope for the future that I hadn't experienced in a long time. I knew that regardless of the state in life God called me to, my story would matter, and He would show me how best to share it with the world. I had no idea what direction that would take but was so excited to find out.

~ ~ ~

I could write pages upon pages of the wonders the Lord has worked in my life since that fateful day. These would include becoming a middle school religion teacher, meeting my husband during a global pandemic, and starting an online ministry—none of which I ever would have anticipated. But as I've been reminded recently, God often works in our lives in ways we'd least expect. For years, I tried to force my life to work out the way I wanted it to, hurting myself and others in the process. Yet even in my wanderings, the Lord never released His hold on me. He found me time and time again, and now He's sent me on a mission to find others. To find you.

INTO LIGHT

In Genesis 1:1–5, we read that the world was in darkness. Though I'm no scripture scholar, I like to think the Lord allowed this to happen to make it clear from day one that He alone is the source of all light. Without Him, the world would have remained in darkness; without Him, there would be no light. And, without the darkness, we wouldn't know what light was. Without sadness, there would be no joy.

There's a moment in *Inside Out* where Bing Bong, Riley's imaginary friend, is forced to face the fact that he will soon fade into forgottenness. Seeing him distraught by this frightful truth, Joy tries to make Bing Bong feel better by bringing to his mind all the good times he and Riley have shared. In other words, she tries to force him to rejoice with her. When Bing Bong doesn't respond to her efforts, Joy walks away defeated, baffled by her inability to help her hurting friend. She is even more taken aback when Bing Bong opens up to Sadness, who, rather than try to force Bing Bong to be happy when he's hurting, is content to simply sit with him and support him by her presence—and, ultimately, to weep with him.

This brings to mind the image of Jesus in the garden of Gethsemane the night before His Passion. He was not only enveloped in physical darkness; He also experienced intense spiritual desolation. He knew what the next day would bring, and though He knew it was going to bring about the greatest good imaginable, He still trembled in fear. I find it interesting that He rallied His friends around Him at that time. Surely, just having them close soothed His heart, knowing He wasn't alone. Though I felt alone in my sin for years, one friend's courage to speak out broke through my darkness. She turned my sadness into joy, my despair into hope, and encouraged me to persevere on the path to healing. I wouldn't be writing this book if it wasn't for her.

My journey of restoration has included many professional counseling sessions. It has included countless confessions, and it has borne more tears than I knew could be produced by the human body. But above all, it has brought peace to my soul. It has brought forgiveness, both for those who've hurt me and for myself. Finally, it has given me a mission to share my joy and hope with you that you may find freedom. I hope to inspire you to do the same.

Have you seen *The Passion of the Christ?* I will never forget the ending: the screen is shrouded in the darkness of the grave, and death seems to have had the last word. Suddenly, a light shines forth, and you see Jesus. The cloth He was buried in fades away, and all You see is His face. His eyes are closed. He seems to be in contemplation. Counting. Waiting.

Not only was Jesus thinking of you when He rose from the grave, but He was thinking of each and every one of your wounds and exactly when and how the power of His Resurrection would heal them. Maybe not today, maybe not tomorrow, but in His perfect timing, you will experience healing. You will experience freedom. You will experience victory. If you give Christ permission to restore you to glory, He will give you the grace to see through your wounds into the future—a future full of hope.

Your new life is waiting for you. Christ is waiting for you. He's inviting you to come, just as you are, joys and sorrows alike. He's inviting you to come out of hiding so that you can be healed.

Let's step into the light together, shall we?

ACKNOWLEDGEMENTS

First and foremost, thank You, Father in heaven, for the gift of my life and those of all Your children. Without a single one of us, the world would be a darker place. Thank You for Your light.

Thank you, Mother Mary, for wrapping me and my story in your mantle. My only desire is to please you and emulate you in all I say and do. May this work be a testament to that truth.

Thank you to my friend Amber Colvis. If you hadn't stepped in and saved the day, this story would have remained in darkness. Thank you for believing in it and in me. Thank you Shirley Klump, Sylvia Spicer, and Allison Balderrama, who also took the time to read and edit the manuscript in its beginning stages.

Special thanks to Grace Malinee, who slaved over my manuscript and pushed me to be the best writer I could be. As He knows full well, Grace, I owe you everything.

I would also like to thank my spiritual mentor, Tiffany O'Neill, and friend, Erin Henninger. Whether you knew it or not, your stories, witnesses, and prayers were the final push I needed.

Thank you, Covenant Books, for publishing my work. Special thanks to Sheree Pruett for her kindness and Ben Kerchner for his attentiveness to this project. Thank you for seeing my story as worthy of sharing with the world.

To my beloved husband, Casey—words can never say thank you enough. Before I met you, I did not know what true love was. Thank you for respecting me, loving me, and helping me see the woman God has made me to be. Without you, I would not have found Covenant Books when I did and would not be sharing my story now. Thank you for taking this leap of faith with me and never giving up on us. You are my happy ending.

Finally, thank you to everyone whose story is intertwined in these pages, especially my family and friends. In darkness or light, sadness or joy, you were there, and you have changed my life—for good. I hope I have done the same for you.

CHAPTER 1 REFLECTION QUESTIONS

- What stood out to you most from this chapter?
- What is the first thing that comes to mind when you hear the terms "dark" and "light"?
- Do you believe the world was in darkness at the very beginning? Why do you think God allowed it to be this way?
- Have you experienced darkness in your life? Did you feel close to God or far away from Him during this time? Share this experience with someone you love and trust.
- What emotion(s) do you experience most often? Why do you think that is? If you tend to experience a lot of "negative" emotions, who is someone with whom you can share these things?
- Recommended for listening:
    - "Find Me Here," Simple Offering
    - "Way Maker," Leeland
    - "Lord, I Need You," Matt Maher

CHAPTER 2 REFLECTION QUESTIONS

- What stood out to you most from this chapter?
- When in your life have you felt abandoned? What was that experience like?
- What was your first experience of grief? Share this time with someone you love.
- Many people question God's existence during difficult times. Have you ever doubted God's existence? If so, what led you to question it? Are you still unsure now?
- When have you had to lean on God and trust in His plan, even if you didn't understand it?
- Recommended for listening:
  - "Even in the Silence (Live) [feat. Simple Offering]," NOVUM COLLECTIVE
  - "Know You (feat. Steffany Gretzinger)," Koryn Hawthorne
  - "Let It Be," The Beatles

CHAPTER 3 REFLECTION QUESTIONS

- What stood out to you most from this chapter?
- Would you like to be a saint? Why or why not?
- What does the world or your culture teach about chastity? What is God's vision for it?
- Have you ever sinned against yourself? If so, take some time to journal or pray out loud a prayer of forgiveness.
- Have you received the sacrament of reconciliation? If you've never confessed serious sins, ask the Holy Spirit to give you the courage to do so. If you haven't been to confession in a long time, ask the Lord to place someone in your life who can help you make the journey back to the sacrament.
- Recommended for listening:
    - "The Saint That Is Just Me," Danielle Rose
    - "O Come to the Altar (Live)," Elevation Worship
    - "Who You Say I Am," Hillsong Worship

CHAPTER 4 REFLECTION QUESTIONS

- What stood out to you most from this chapter?
- Are you currently dating someone? If so, why are you with this person? Even if you aren't in a relationship but are interested in dating, it's good to reflect on why you desire it. It can be helpful to discuss these things with a priest, a spiritual director, or other wise mentors who can see your interior motivations more clearly than you and advise you accordingly.
- Have you committed sins against chastity with another person? If so, have you asked God to forgive you? Have you asked the person to forgive you? Even if they've hurt you too, hearing "I forgive you" is an incredibly powerful and important part of the healing process.
- Do you struggle to forgive yourself? Are you having a hard time moving on after a breakup? If so, I encourage you to consider professional counseling. This played a pivotal part in my healing journey. Some schools and workplaces offer free counseling, but if they don't, insurance might cover all or part of the cost. I recommend going to someone who is Catholic and in good standing with the Church.
- Recommended for listening:
    - "Prodigal Child," Simple Offering
    - "I Am No Victim," Kristene DiMarco
    - "Run to the Father," Cody Carnes

CHAPTER 5 REFLECTION QUESTIONS

- What stood out to you most from this chapter?
- Describe a time in your life when someone stepped in to help you even though you didn't expect them to. Did you thank the person?
- Simon of Cyrene was forced to help Jesus carry the cross on the way to Calvary. Has there been an instance when you felt forced to help someone? Were you a willing or a reluctant Simon?
- Have you offered to pray with anyone before? If so, what was that experience like? If you've never been prayed with and would like to be, ask the Holy Spirit to send someone to you with His healing touch.
- Have you prayed with anyone before? Ask the Holy Spirit to reveal who you can pray for this week.
- Recommended for listening:
  - "Rescue," Lauren Daigle
  - "New Wine," Hillsong Worship
  - "Look What You've Done," Tasha Layton

CHAPTER 6 REFLECTION QUESTIONS

- What stood out to you most from this chapter?
- Have you ever felt called to do something by God? This could be as small as smiling at someone or as big as writing a book. Whatever it was, how did you respond? What was the outcome?
- Have you ever been afraid of what God is asking of you? What is the worst that could happen? What is the best? What are you waiting for?
- Who have you seen doing something great for God? What inspires you most about that person?
- If nothing was stopping you—even your own fear—what would you want to do with your life? Invite God into that, and close with a prayer, surrendering yourself completely to Him. Trust that He will take care of everything.
- Recommended for listening:
  - "Lead of Love," Caedmon's Call
  - "Pieces," Amanda Lindsey Cook
  - "Too Good to Not Believe," Cody Carnes & Brandon Lake

CHAPTER 7 REFLECTION QUESTIONS

- What stood out to you most from this chapter?
- Make a list of some of the most challenging times in your life. Ask the Holy Spirit to be with you and to lead you in this process. It is dangerous to journey into our wounds without Him. Then share at least one thing from your list with a trusted friend, parent, guardian, priest, teacher, youth minister, counselor, spouse, etc. How does this make you feel?
- While we are called to "weep with those who weep," we are also called to "rejoice with those who rejoice." Take your list of hardships and separate each one onto its own page. Then ask the Holy Spirit to show you how He has shone light into this time of darkness. If you can't think of anything, ask your friend or loved one to help you. Invite that person to be the light of Christ for you. Allow yourself to be found, and praise God for loving you, fighting for you, and working things for your good, even when you couldn't see it.
- Recommended for listening:
  - "Out of Hiding," Steffany Gretzinger
  - "Catch Me Singing," Sean Curran
  - "Seasons," Hillsong Worship

CHASTITY COMMITMENT CARD

~ True Love Waits ~

I make a commitment to God, myself, my family, my friends, those
I date, my future spouse and children, and all those I encounter
that I will always seek to live a life of chastity—as a single person,
in religious life, or within a covenant marriage relationship.

Name ____

____

Date ____________________________________

ABOUT THE AUTHOR

Morgan Swartz is an engaging Catholic speaker and founder of *Joyinhope*. She earned a bachelor of arts in theology from Benedictine College in 2018. Since then, she has spent time in religious education, youth ministry, and young adult ministry. She currently resides in Kansas with her husband and son.

Joyinhope features videos, podcasts, and a blog on various Christian topics. Morgan's mission is to bring light to the dark by creating content that uplifts and inspires people to live happier, holier lives. In addition to this ministry, Morgan travels the world speaking at retreats and conferences, sharing her love for the Lord.

www.ingramcontent.com/pod-product-compliance
Lightning Source LLC
Chambersburg PA
CBHW031417160726
47993CB00003B/1282